Profound Leadership Principles

People ... Priority One!

Profound. Synonyms include heartfelt, intense, sincere, wholehearted, or even deep-seated.

Fifty years in leadership roles have allowed me to formulate strong, heartfelt beliefs about leadership. Anyone aspiring to and actively involved as a leader can never take the role casually. It's a tremendous opportunity with immense responsibility.

Leaders influence and impact people's lives -- either for better or worse. There doesn't seem to be a middle ground. Every action, interaction, or decision will leave residue that enhances or detracts from people's ability to perform and their impression of the leader.

Profound Leadership Principles are powerful, practical, thought-provoking statements, and quotes that every leader wrestles with or at least those who are serious about positively influencing the work culture, team effectiveness, and personal impact.

Keep in mind, these are principles, not suggested strategies. Strategies can change, be modified, or fluctuate based on current circumstances. Principles don't change. Regardless of what's going on in the moment, principles remain solidly embedded in a leader's attitude and action.

I hope you will find this accumulation of Profound Leadership Principles to be inspirational, real-time, and a boost to your leadership confidence.

Blessings... Glenn Van Ekeren

When leaders love people more than paper, policies, or profit... passion permeates the culture.

"Leadership is all about the people. It is not about organizations. It is not about plans. It is not about strategies. It is all about people motivating people to get the job done. You have to be people centered."

- Colin Powell

Be more concerned with what people can become than with what they do.

"My job is not to be easy on people. My job is to take these great people we have and push them and make them even better."

- Steve Jobs

You can help people become more of who they are, but you can't make them something they're not.

Help people become more of who they are.

"Leadership is communicating people's worth and potential so convincingly that they are inspired to see it in themselves."

- Stephen Covey

People don't respond progressively better when being treated progressively worse.

"The challenge of leadership is to be strong but not rude; be kind, but not weak; be bold, but not a bully; be humble, but not timid; be proud, but not arrogant; have humor, but without folly."

- Jim Rohn

Taking people to the top is unimaginable unless you're on the journey yourself.

"The purpose of leadership is to take others to the top."

- John Maxwell

Leadership begins with our ability to get inside of another person's world and to see it as they see it, not how we think they see it.

It's not what you think.
It's not what you think people think.
It's what they think that really matters.

"In environments in which human needs are acknowledged and talent and creativity are allowed to flourish, employees give their all."

- Charles Garfield

People are a valuable, appreciating asset only if we are willing to invest in them.

"Employees who don't feel significant rarely make significant contributions."

- Mark Sanborn

Leadership Paradox:

The more control a leader attempts to force on people, the more control they lose.

"It's horrifying how easy it is to de-motivate someone --
to dent/diminish/destroy their fragile psychological ownership of a task!"

- Tom Peters

People do things for their reasons, not your reasons. People do things because they want to, not because you think it would be a good idea.

Find their reason!

"Everyone is special.
Everyone has special needs and desires.
The one trick is to find out what those needs are. Then if you treat people special –
if you help them get what they want –
you can't help but succeed."

- Lou Holtz

Leaders inspire people to become a better version of who they are.

"Leadership is about making others better as a result of your presence and making sure that impact lasts in your absence."

- Sheryl Sandberg

It doesn't make sense to hire smart people and then have them follow stupid rules.

"The bigger the 'policy and procedures' manual, the duller the company. Innovation and entrepreneurship go down as the number of policies go up."

- Jeffrey J. Fox

Hire people who other companies want to hire. Treat them in a way they would never want to leave.

"Surround yourself with the best people you can find, delegate authority, and don't interfere."

- Ronald Reagan

Visionary (future focused) leadership is NOT a "Nice-ity" - - - **it is a necessity.**

"The future belongs to those who see the possibilities before they become obvious."

- John Sculley

Consistent inconsistency is the most consistent form of consistency.

"There is nothing so unequal as the equal treatment of unequals."

- Vince Lombardi

Don't let what's considered normal stop you from creating a new normal or even better, abnormal.

"The inspiration to generate ideas comes easy, but the inspiration to take action is more rare."

- Scott Belsky

Growing leaders grow people. Stagnant leaders stagnate people. Growing companies require growing leaders.

"If we can build an environment in which people can learn and grow, the grass will not be greener on the other side."

- Libby Sartain

Mission is a power producing, directional tool that gives people the "**why**" behind the "**what**".

"If people relate to the company they work for, if they form an emotional tie to it and buy into its dreams, they will pour their heart into making it better."

- Howard Schultz

Vision...

You don't need certainty on how to get there, just clarity on where you plan to go.

"Before we can build great companies, we have to imagine them. Great work always starts with a great vision of the future."

- Simon Sinek

Create an environment where people feel good about themselves, the people they work with, the people they serve, and go home feeling good about the organization.

"Every leader will establish a culture – either **intentional** or **unintentional**."

- Dr. Tom Osborne

Never
ever – ever – ever – ever
hire the best of the worst!

"You cannot push anyone
up a ladder unless he is
willing to climb a little."

- Andrew Carnegie

If the status quo
was painful,
people would have
challenged it already.

"Beware the lollipop of mediocrity;
lick it once and you'll suck forever."

- Brian Wilson

Better players make better players better.

"If you are settling for mediocrity, it is time to stop dog paddling as you tread water and start rocking the boat."

— Dave Anderson

Engagement

You can't force it, but you can create a culture that nourishes it.

"If you are lucky enough to be someone's employer then you have a moral obligation to make sure people do look forward to coming to work in the morning."

- John Mackey

"If your people are headed in the wrong direction, don't motivate them."

- George Odiorne

Jumpstarting people's performance requires expanding a person's view of themselves and helping them grow beyond their self-imposed limitations.

If you retired today, would you be remembered as a leader who embraced the future and continually refined your image of what the future would look like?

Or, remembered as the one who fell in love with the status quo and warmly allowed others to do the same?

"The status quo sets on society like fat on cold chicken soup, and it is quite content to be what it is. Unless someone comes along to stir things up, there just won't be change."

- Abbie Hoffman

If you're as good as you're going to be, you don't deserve to be the leader.

"We expect our leaders
to be better than we are,
or why are we following them."

- Paul Harvey

Never Allow Circumstances to Dictate Quality

"Be a yardstick of quality. Some people aren't used to an environment where excellence is expected."

- Steve Jobs

Be The Team Others Aspire to Be

"People are more inclined to be drawn in if their leader has a compelling vision. Great leaders help people get in touch with their own aspirations and then will help them forge those aspirations into a personal vision."

- John Kotter

Be someone who makes someone else look forward to tomorrow.

"You get the best effort from others not by lighting a fire beneath them, but by building a fire within them."

— Bob Nelson

If the communicator is unable to communicate clearly, the hearer will be unable to comprehend clearly.

"If it's a mist in the pulpit, it will be a fog in the pew."

- Howard Hendricks

Leaders, begin each day asking:

"What can I do today to set people up for success?"

"How can I speak life, hope, and confidence into someone?"

"Outstanding leaders go out of the way to boost the self-esteem of their personnel. If people believe in themselves, it's amazing what they can accomplish."

— Sam Walton

Never do anything for anybody they can do for themselves.

"Our chief want in life, is someone who will make us do what we can."

- Ralph Waldo Emerson

Outstanding Performance...

You have to expect it before you can get it.

"If you want people who work for you to strive for their best possible performance, give them as much responsibility as they can handle. Give them room to breathe and develop and hold them accountable for what they do."

- Buck Rogers

Caution:
Routine can result in careless execution.

"The thing that keeps a business ahead of the competition is excellence in execution."

- Tom Peters

Develop people's strengths and strengthen their weakness.

"The real difference between success and failure in a corporation can very often be traced to the question of how well the organization brings out the energies and talents of its people."

- Thomas J. Watson

If my team doesn't believe in me and what I represent, they won't believe in what I want to do or where I dream the organization can go.

"If you want outstanding results from people who work for you, you need to make a personal connection with them. Team members want a personal connection with their supervisor. Being a figurehead will never inspire people to follow you."

- James Kouses and Barry Posner

Visionary leaders create
a culture that
celebrates newness…

the search for what's "just right."

"The leader has the
responsibility to come up
above the trees periodically
and refresh the vision
and make sure that
they've looked at the
landscape as if they've
never seen it before."

- Cheryl Bachelder

Leaders who make "love" a verb often find that others treat them the same way.

"Leadership comes down to taking care of the people in your organization and making them the best they can be, not giving up on them, and never failing to be there for them."

- Pete Carroll

You can't lead people to where you haven't been.

Your people can only grow as far as you've grown.

"A leader takes people where they want to go. A great leader takes people where they don't necessarily want to go, but ought to be."

- Rosalynn Carter

"How you select people is more important than how you manage them once they're on the job. If you start with the right people, you won't have problems later on. If you hire the wrong people… you're in serious trouble."

- Red Auerbach

Hiring recklessly or randomly results in repetitious remorse.

When we think about the special people in our lives, let this be the second golden rule:

- - -

Remember the best, let go of the rest!

"Personal relationships are the fertile soil from which all advancement, all success, all achievement in real life grow."

- Ben Stein

Leaders are responsible TO
help people make their lives better…
NOT FOR making their lives better.

"Leaders aren't responsible for the results. They are responsible for the people; who are responsible for the results."

- Simon Sinek

Be the leader you would love your children to work for.

"One of the most fundamental lessons of leadership is that if you're a leader, it's not about you. It's about the people following you. The best leaders devote almost all their energy to inspiring and enabling others. Taking care of them is a big part of this."

— George Bradt

Recruitment isn't an activity.

Recruitment is a way of life.

"First-rate people hire first-rate people;
second-rate people hire third-rate people."

- Leo Rosten

The way to keep good people around is to keep good people around good people.

"The wrong people are your greatest catastrophe, and mediocre people are your greatest drain on resource."

\- Dave Anderson

Don't be infected...
be contagious!

"As a leader, your attitude doesn't just affect your day, it affects everyone around you also."

- Kurt Uhlir

People aren't searching for rules to live by but a purpose to live for.

"People want to be part of **something larger than themselves**. They want to be part of something they're really proud of, that they'll fight for, sacrifice for, that they trust."

- Howard Schultz, Starbucks

Provide a healthy, upbeat, optimistic, and positive example of what you want the culture to be.

*"The three most important
ways to lead people are:
by example...
by example...
by example."*

- Albert Schweitzer

Create a culture where people believe they can perform better than they thought possible.

"Leadership is lifting a person's vision to high sights, raising a person's performance to a higher standard, building a personality beyond its normal limitations."

- Peter Drucker

Managers know how to light a fire, but leaders know how to keep it burning.

"You can't manufacture passion or "motivate" people to feel passionate. You can only discover what ignites your passion and the passions of those around you."

- Jim Collins

You can't STANDARDIZE people's attitudes.

"Lead and inspire people. Don't try to manage and manipulate people. Inventories can be managed but people must be led."

— Ross Perot

Where there are no consequences for poor performance, the wrong actions will continue.

Where there is no reinforcement for desirable performance, the behavior will cease.

"In the end, as a leader, you are always going to get a combination of two things: what you create and what you allow."

- Henry Cloud

People won't believe in, get passionate about, or pursue a vision, unless they believe in the leader.

"When the things you say and the things you do are in alignment with what you actually believe, a thriving culture emerges."

- Simon Sinek

Leaders who don't get carried away… should be.

"To have long-term success as a coach or in any position of leadership, you have to be obsessed in some way."

- Pat Riley

Leaders have the awesome privilege to be relentless architects of people's future.

"A leader's role is to raise people's aspirations for what they can become and to release their energies so they will try to get there."

- David Gergen

Leaders must become passionate lunatics in communicating their heart and then make sure they follow through to passionately ensure implementation.

"Your passion gives permission to those around you to express theirs."

- Brad Lomenick

People development is what's usually done when there is time left over.

Never let the tyranny of the urgent take priority over people.

"Leadership is being a faithful, devoted, hard-working servant of the people you lead and participating with them in the agonies as well as the ecstasies of life."

- Herb Kelleher

Trust

Leaders go first.

Trust until people prove themselves untrustworthy!

Not trusting everyone has no effect on those who can't be trusted but has a debilitating effect on those who can be trusted.

"If you mistrust your employees, you'll be right three percent of the time. If you trust people until they give you a reason not to, you'll be right 97 percent of the time."

- Wolf J. Rinke

A dynamic leader is someone you will follow to a place you wouldn't go by yourself.

"If your actions inspire others to dream more, learn more, and become more, you are a leader."

- John Quincy Adams

Leadership shines brightest when the leader does what nobody else is willing to do.

"If you're not willing to do things that others would say are over the top, and if you're not comfortable being criticized for being annoying and for having standards that seem perhaps just a little too high, then you'll drift toward mediocrity."

- Patrick Lencioni

The more team members know,
the more they understand;
the more they understand,
the more they care.

"Communication builds trust.
Trust generates commitment.
Commitment fosters teamwork,
and teamwork delivers great results."

- Jon Gordon

People look to the leader to be who they expect others to be.

"Leadership is being the first egg in the omelet."

- Jarod Kintz

Rule driven leaders love to produce rules to keep everyone from doing what only a few people are doing, and they plan to keep doing it regardless of the rules.

"Rules are made for people who aren't willing to make up their own."

- Brigadier General Chuck Yeager

Today's hiring mistakes are tomorrow's turnover.

"People are not your most important asset. The right people are."

- Jim Collins

If your team was just like you, would you be proud of them?

"The people on your team expect you to be upbeat, positive, confident, and certain they can win."

- Coach Mike Krzyzewski

What's an unthinkable thing to do right now in your world? If you could pull it off, would it dramatically change the quality of what you do?

Do It!

"Perhaps more than anything else, leadership is about the 'creation of a new way of life'."

- James M. Kouzes & Barry Z. Posner

"When a leader fails to expect enough, he thwarts his people's potential, shrinks their thinking, narrows their vision, and conditions them to mediocrity until average becomes acceptable."

- Dave Anderson

Impressive, jaw-dropping, incredible, and impressive results rarely grow out of marginal expectations.

"A good leader takes
a little more than his
share of the blame,
a little less than his
share of the credit."

- Arnold Glasow

See what's right with people and say something.

If there is nothing new, innovative, challenging, or paradigm shifting going on in your head, there is nothing freshly inspiring coming out of your mouth.

"Creativity is inventing, experimenting, growing, taking risks, breaking rules, making mistakes, and having fun."

- Mary Lou Cook

Complimentary people
are complimented by those
they compliment with a heightened
desire to earn the compliment they received.

"You never know when a moment and
a few sincere words can have an
impact on a life."

- Zig Ziglar

"People tend to resist that which is forced upon them. People tend to support that which they help to create."

—Vince Pfaff

Involvement breeds commitment and commitment breeds a spirit of ownership.

Likeability is not the result of making everyone happy but genuinely acting in people's best interest.

"Although being likeable is not a guarantee that people will follow you, it is certainly a factor; being unlikeable, on the other hand, is an almost certain guarantee that people will not follow you."

- Jeb Blount

Transparency communicates the message to hold me accountable to be who I say I will be and do what I say I will do.

"To be a good boss, you must be transparent. There's a correlation between worker happiness and workplace transparency. Leaders and managers who offer transparency will earn the respect and devotion of their team."

- David Niu

Get comfortable in your skin and understand how others see your complexion.

"Don't paint stripes on your back if you're not a zebra. Focus on building upon your unique abilities."

- Lee J. Colan

As leaders, we are called to enliven people's spirits, see the possibilities, and provide hope when circumstances are grim.

"Practice bringing a calm to chaos, clarity to the unknown, and confidence to uncertain circumstances."

- Brad Lomenick

Make where you work a place where people love to be!

"A healthy company is immediately noticeable. Employees 'bounce' into work, they are interested in their jobs...and they go home feeling good about themselves and their accomplishments."

- Robert Reed

Treat everyone as the most important person in your life.

"Treat people greatly; they will show themselves great."

- Ralph Waldo Emerson

"I'm sorry I was wrong."

- - -

Speaks to your integrity...
and humility.

"Abandon the old-fashioned notion that it is a sign of weakness for a manager or leader to apologize."

- James Autry

"I believe it's clear...
CRYSTAL CLEAR...
that people are attracted to...
and retained by...
institutions that...
MAKE THEM FEEL GOOD
ABOUT THEMSELVES AS
HUMAN BEINGS."

– Tom Peters

Become the kind of leader people would follow even if you didn't have a title.

Never allow the world to determine your attitude but allow your attitude to impact the world.

"I guarantee as a leader no one will ever be more optimistic than you are. But if you are a pessimist, I can almost equally guarantee that they will be more pessimistic than you are."

- Richard Lenny
EO Hershey Foods

Who I am, how I act, and what I stand for as a leader sets the expectation for the team.

"Make your personal standard of performance - your behavior in all areas so exemplary that those under your supervision will find it hard to match, harder to surpass."

- John Wooden

Do anything to help people be successful except lower the standard.

"I would rather perform at 90 percent of an excellence standard than 110 percent of an adequacy standard."

- Don Beveridge

Fight the policy pandemic!
Eradicate them... **now!**

Establish policies for the majority, not the minority.

"Leaders are not
obsessed with rules.
Any fool can make a rule."

- Henry David Thoreau

Our people expect us to be upbeat, positive, and confident, or otherwise why should they be?

"If you're working in a company that is not ENTHUSIASTIC, energetic, creative, clever, curious, and just plain fun, you've got troubles, serious troubles."

- Tom Peters

Tell your team everything so you're not accused of not telling them something.

"The problem with communication is the illusion that it has been accomplished."

- George Bernard Shaw

Be tough minded on standards and tender hearted on people.

"Compassion without accountability produces sentimentalism. Accountability without compassion is harsh and heartless. **Compassion teamed up with accountability is a powerful force** – one which we have found can provide a great incentive to excel."

— John D. Beckett

Hire people you would like your kids to work with.

"If you are going to hire someone that doesn't have character, you had better hope they are dumb and lazy or they will do a lot of stupid things."

-Warren Buffet

"People and rubber bands have one thing in common: they must be stretched to be effective."

- John Maxwell

If you aren't growing somewhere, you aren't going anywhere!

One of the realities of leadership is to be unpopular when it is necessary.

"Some managers should wear bonnets and carry diaper bags, because in their management role, they function more as a nanny than as a leader."

- Dave Anderson

Leaders give up their right to attend "ain't it awful" happy hours, moan and groan sessions, pity parties, againstovist meetings and negativer conventions.

"Leadership is a matter of how to be, not how to do."

- Frances Hesselbein

Good people deserve to work with good people.

"Any business or industry that pays equal rewards to its goof-offs and its eager beavers sooner or later will find itself with more goof-offs than eager beavers."

— Mick Delaney

You cannot build a world class organization with marginal people.

"Everyone you meet is a potential winner; some are disguised as losers. Don't be fooled by their appearances."

- Ken Blanchard

Close-minded leaders close minds.

"Whatever you do in life, surround yourself with smart people who'll argue with you."

- John Wooden

Unified teams will figure out the right thing to do at the right time in the right way for the right reasons.

"A united culture is a harmonious one that is open to 'difference'. A uniform culture, in which everyone is the same, will suffocate innovation."

- Jackie & Kevin Freiberg

"Learn how to separate the majors and the minors. A lot of people don't do well simply because they major in the minors."

- Jim Rohn

Don't major in the minors or minor in the majors.

Process... Process... Process...

It's not WHAT you do but HOW you do it.

"By treating people right, they will do right for you."

— Laszlo Bock

The moment you take responsibility for everything in your life is the moment you can change something in your life.

"There are two primary choices in life:
to accept conditions as they exist, or accept
the responsibility for changing them."

- Denis Waitley

Without Vision, Strategy is Worthless.
Without Strategy, Execution is Aimless.
Without Execution, Vision is Useless.
Without Culture, it is All Meaningless.

"It takes a leader to create the momentum, it takes a vision to direct the momentum, it takes a massive action to build on the momentum, and it takes self-discipline to sustain the momentum."

- Farshad Asl

No one leaves an organization because leadership communicates too much.

"The two words 'information' and 'communication' are often used interchangeably, but they signify quite different things. Information is giving out; communication is getting through."

- Sydney J. Harris

"Before you ever utter a word,
the team sees your face,
the look in your eyes, even your walk.
Show the face your team needs to see."

- Coach Mike Krzyzewski

Leaders are the pulse

---

the heartbeat of
the organization.

Leaders are defined not by what they believe but how they live what they say they believe.

"Leadership is a matter of having people look at you and gain confidence seeing how you react. If you're in control, they're in control."

- Tom Landry

Ride the White Horse

–

Take the High Road

–

When you get even with people, it makes you even with those you don't like.

"One of the toughest things for leaders to master is kindness. Kindness shares credit and offers enthusiastic praise for others' work. It's a balancing act between being genuinely kind and not looking weak."

- Travis Bradberry

What got you where you are won't get you where you want to go.

Challenge what is!

"If in the last few years you haven't discarded a major opinion or acquired a new one, check your pulse.
You may be dead."

- Gelett Burgess

"The Leader is the servant who removes the obstacles that prevent people from doing their jobs."

- Max De Pree

Teams need "A" level processes where "C" level people can get "A" level results.

You can achieve
world class results,
or
you can make excuses,
but you can't do both.

"Once your excuses are gone, you'll simply have to settle for being awesome."

- Lorii Myers

"Help me understand…"

"I only wish I could find an institute that teaches people how to listen. Business people need to listen at least as much as they need to talk. Too many people fail to realize that real communication goes both directions."

- Lee Iacocca

Stupid mistake.
Let's have lunch.

"There are three kinds of men: The one that learns by reading. The few who learn by observation. The rest of them have to pee on the electric fence for themselves."

- Will Rogers

You, as a leader, don't inspire your team by showing them how wonderful you are but how incredible they are.

"A leader's role is to raise people's aspirations for what they can become and to release their energies so they will try to get there."

- David Gergen

If everyone led the way you do, would the world be a better place?

"Shine your light and make a positive impact on the world; there is nothing so honorable as helping improve the lives of others."

- Roy T. Bennett

"If you don't have a vision, you're going to be stuck in what you know. And the only thing you know is what you've already seen."

- Iyanla Vanzant

You will never leave where you are until you decide where you would rather be.

When sacred cows are eradicated, exponential results are possible!

Until sacred cows are eradicated, incremental improvements are the limit.

"I've always challenged myself and the people who work with me to take new approaches to traditional business challenges, to push the envelope, and constantly ask whether our sacred cows are still producing great milk."

- Irene Rosenfeld

"Establishing a habit of excellence begins with a core commitment to set a standard that scares the daylights out of you."

- Brad Lomenick

When challenging the status quo becomes the status quo,
we no longer have to think about challenging the status quo.

To be extraordinary,
stop being ordinary….

        If you want to be uncommon,
        quit being common…

If you want to be remarkable,
quit being predictable…

        If you want to be radically
        different, eliminate
        the status quo.

"You never change your life until you step out of your comfort zone; change begins at the end of your comfort zone."

- Roy T. Bennett

Pursue the unthinkable so you can achieve the unimaginable.

"Vision without action is merely a dream. Action without vision just passes the time. Vision with action can change the world."

- Joel Barker

"Always seek to excel yourself. Put yourself in competition with yourself each day. Each morning look back upon your work of yesterday and then try to beat it."

- Charles M. Sheldon

"To each of us at certain points of our lives, there come opportunities to rearrange our formulas and assumptions, not necessarily to rid of the old, but more to profit from adding something new."

- Leo Buscaglia

The challenge is often NOT generating new, innovative ideas, but rather burying old ones.

"Every organization has to prepare for the abandonment of everything it does."

- Peter Drucker

Create a strategic – stop-doing plan.

"Nobody can go back and start a new beginning, but anyone can start today and make a new ending."

- Maria Robinson

"It's not the magic that makes it work; it's the way we work that makes it magic."

- Lee Cockerell

It's not the work we do but how we do the work that creates "WOW" experiences in people's lives.

When you change your view of the world, the possibilities inside your world will change.

"If you don't like something, change it. If you can't change it, change the way you think about it."

- Mary Engelbreit

"I used to believe that culture was 'soft,' and had little bearing on our bottom line. What I believe today is that our culture has everything to do with our bottom line, now and into the future."

- Vern Dosch

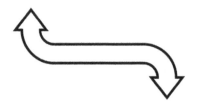

If you don't get the soft stuff right, it is difficult to achieve the hard stuff for the long term.

The culture of any team is shaped by the worst behavior the leader is willing to tolerate.

"The fundamental keys to the culture of any organization can only be achieved when everyone is on the same page."

- Tony Dungy

If you want people to be
what you are,
then be what you want
them to be.

"Be who you say you are, and your team will become what you want them to be."

- Mark Sanborn

You can't grow by becoming more ordinary or predictable. **Seek remarkable. Be original!** Whether intentional or accidental, break the monotonous mold of mediocrity by embracing a world class journey.

"Leaders are fascinated by the future. You are a leader if and only if, you are restless for change, impatient for progress, and deeply dissatisfied with the status quo. Because in your head, you can see a better future. The friction between 'what is' and 'what could be' burns you, stirs you up, propels you. This is leadership."

- Marcus Buckingham

Closed-minded leaders don't know they are closed minded because they are closed minded.

"The leader must be interested in finding the best way, not in having his own way."

- John Wooden

Deliver tough news first.
Then move to an upbeat message.
Get the bad stuff over with and then move on.
"Bad news isn't wine.
It doesn't improve with age."

- Colin Powell

Do what you do like no one else does it.

"Doing the best at this moment puts you in the best place for the next moment."

- Oprah Winfrey

Quality cannot occur in an adversarial environment... world class thrives in an environment of collaboration.

"If everyone is moving forward together, then success takes care of itself."

- Henry Ford

Team Members cannot see the Vision in your Head...
Communicate...
Communicate...
Communicate...

"Good business leaders create a vision, articulate the vision, passionately own the vision, and relentlessly drive it to completion."

- Jack Welch

If serving is below you, leadership is above you.

"Use power to help people. For we are given power not to advance our own purposes or to make a great show in the world, nor a name. There is but one just use of power and it is to serve people."

- George Bush
1989 Inaugural Speech

Believe in people more than they believe in themselves.

"Men and women want to do a good job, a creative job, and if they are provided the proper environment, they will do so."

~ Bill Hewlett

"The true test of the effectiveness of the leader is this: Are your people better off when they leave than when they arrived?"

- James C. Hunter

People don't bust their buns for just anyone

\- - -

Give the best of you to them.

Be more concerned with what people can become than with what they do.

"My job is **not** to be easy on people. My job is to take these great people we have and push them and make them even better."

- Steve Jobs

Only those who settle for mediocrity are always at their best.

"Don't settle for mediocrity. Take a chance. Take a risk. Find that passion. Rekindle it. Fall in love all over again. It's really worth it."

- Bryan Cranston

Most people who are fired were hired wrong.

"Hiring the right people takes time, the right questions and a healthy dose of curiosity. What do you think is the most important factor when building your team? For us, it's personality."

- Richard Branson

It is impossible to build a great team around marginal people.

"... you must spend priority time with "<u>**potential**</u>" people. Otherwise, it's like going to a horse race and betting your life savings on a nag, just to improve its self-image; seemingly noble but ultimately stupid."

- Dave Anderson

The more rules you make the more rules there are to break.

"Too many rules get in the way of leadership. They just put you in a box. . . People set rules to keep from making decisions."

- Mike Krzyzewski

We attract people who don't work for us by making our culture attractive to those who are.

"To empower people, let them know they matter.
Let them know they are valued.
Let them know how important their contribution is to the mission of the organization."

- Kevin Graham Ford & James Osterhaus

Without a clear vision, "what is" is as good as it gets.

"A vision is not just a picture of what could be; it is an appeal to our better selves, a call to become something more."

- Rosabeth Moss Kanter

"You cannot demonstrate that you care electronically. You must build personal relationships with your people. Answering the basic human relations question, "Do you care?" involves a one-on-one expression in person. A handshake and a look in the eyes to say "Thank you" have a far greater impact than any message on a screen."

- David Cottrell

Dynamic leaders care more about people than position.

Ask before
you dictate.

"The quality of a leader cannot be judged by the answers they give but by the questions they ask."

- Simon Sinek

That which we tolerate...
is repeated and often
multiplied.

"It is important that people
know what you stand for.
It's equally important that they
know what you won't stand for."

- Mary Waldrop

If you're as good as
you're going to be,
you shouldn't be the leader.

"The ultimate responsibility of a leader is to facilitate other people's development as well as his own."

- Fred Pryor

You have to expect it before you can get it!

"If I expect great things from my people, they'll go to great lengths to keep from disappointing me."

— John Maxwell

You can't achieve it if you don't see it!

"Average companies give their people something to work on. In contrast, the most innovative organizations give their people something to work toward."

- Simon Sinek

You can hire people to
work <u>for</u> you...

You must understand and attempt to meet their needs in order for them to work <u>with</u> you.

"Leaders know that the
'higher up you go'
- -
the more gently down you reach."

- Sheila Murray Bethel

Sometimes you help people get more out of what they do. Other times you just help them "Get Out" of what they do.

"In the end, as a leader, you are always going to get a combination of two things: what you create and what you allow."

- Dr. Henry Cloud

"Rules are invented for lazy people who don't want to think for themselves."

- Mary Quant
Mother of the Mini Skirt

The immature leader knows the rules. A mature leader understands the exceptions.

Believe in People More Than They Believe in Themselves

Milton Keynes UK
Ingram Content Group UK Ltd.
UKHW052111011124
450603UK00005B/40